explore

wesleyan
publishing
house
Indianapolis, Indiana

Student
book 5
in the Explore Kid's
Discipleship Series

Investigate God's Word
for Yourself

Investigate God's Word for Yourself
Student Book 5 in the Explore Kid's Discipleship Series

Copyright © 2012 by Wesleyan Publishing House
Published by Wesleyan Publishing House
Indianapolis, Indiana 46250
Printed in the United States of America
ISBN: 978-0-89827-591-9

Contributors
Writer: Andrew Bush
Art Director: Kory Pence
Illustrator: Daniel Swartz

www.wesleyan.org/wph

book
5 explore

explore | Investigate God's Word for Yourself

Page

Jesus in Action

The book of Mark is about the good news of Jesus.

Engage

Mark 1:1 says, "This is the Good News about Jesus the Messiah, the Son of God." In the gospel of Mark, the author wanted to show his readers that Jesus was the Messiah they had been waiting for. He wanted to make sure his readers could see the difference between Jesus and all the other prophets God had provided to the Israelite nation.

Check It Out

Acts 2:22–24 summarizes the purpose of the four Gospels, including Mark's.

Read Acts 2:22–24.

I can know it's true:

1. Jesus is the Messiah, God's Son. During the time of Jesus, the Jewish nation was under the rule of the Roman Empire. Hundreds of years before then, God had sent prophets who promised that one day a Messiah would come, set the Jewish nation free, and establish a kingdom that would last forever. Jesus came as the Messiah and established a kingdom that was far greater than any earthly kingdom.

2. Jesus did miracles, wonders, and signs. The gospel of Mark is filled with the actions of Jesus. He performed miracle after miracle and spoke with the authority of God. However, these miracles were not enough to prove that Jesus was the Messiah. There were many prophets before Him that had performed miracles, wonders, and signs of God's power.

3. Jesus was crucified, buried, and raised from the dead! This is what makes Him different from the other prophets. All the other prophets died, but none of them came back to life. This is the good news of Jesus. He did not stay dead. God brought His Son back to life so He could establish a kingdom that would last forever.

Question

John Mark most likely wrote the book of Mark. However, it was Peter who told Mark about the good news of Jesus and what to write.

What other basic facts can you uncover about the book of Mark?

Who: Who was it written to?

What: What makes Mark different?

Where: Where is the book found in the Bible?

When: When did these events take place?

Why: Why was this book written?

Challenge

The challenge this week is to read **Mark 1–3**. As you read, highlight every miracle you find and count how many times the Pharisees caused trouble. Record the number in the circle.
Mark 1:14–15 says, "Later on, after John was arrested

Jesus went into Galilee, where he preached God's Good News. 'The time promised by God has come at last!' he announced. 'The Kingdom of God is near! Repent of your sins and believe the Good News!'"

Underline this passage in your reading this week.

What does it mean to you to repent and believe in the Good News?

The Kingdom of God is near! Repent of your sins and believe the Good News!

—Mark 1:1

Unclean Jesus?

We are called to show compassion to others.

Engage

The man who Jesus healed had leprosy. Jesus taught us a valuable lesson on compassion when He healed this man. Let's take a look and see what happened.

Check It Out
Read Mark 1:40–45.

I can know it's true:

1. Jesus was approached by a man with leprosy. According to the law of Moses, anyone with a skin disease was considered "unclean." That person could not enter towns and was not allowed to be touched by anyone else. This man was "unclean" and rejected by society and felt very lonely. In spite of his bleak situation, the man had faith that Jesus could heal him and make him clean. In our lives, there are many people who are different from us, rejected by society, and lonely. These people are looking for someone to show them the way to Jesus.

2. Jesus saw the man's unfortunate condition and had compassion on him. After all, this man was not even allowed to visit or live with his own family. The sight of this outcast man caused Jesus to feel sorry and have sympathy for him. When we see others in unfortunate situations in life, we should be like Jesus and have compassion on them.

3. Jesus' compassion resulted in action. Jesus' compassion did not end with a sorry feeling. Jesus reached out, touched the man, and healed him! Afterward, Jesus told the man to keep quiet and not spread the news about this miraculous healing. If others found out, they would call Jesus "unclean" and interfere with His ministry. Did the man keep the secret? No! The man was so excited that he told everyone. As a result, Jesus had to stay in secluded places. How incredible it is to think that Jesus touched the leper even though others would consider Him "unclean." We need to follow Jesus' example. Compassion for other people should propel us to action.

Jesus has called us to compassion for others.

Question

Mark 1:41–42 says, "Moved with compassion, Jesus reached out and touched him. 'I am willing,' he said. 'Be healed!' Instantly the leprosy disappeared, and the man was healed."

Why do you think Jesus touched the man with leprosy?

Could Jesus have healed the man without touching him?

How does it make you feel knowing Jesus has compassion on others?

How does it make you feel knowing Jesus has compassion on you?

Who are some people in your life who need your compassion?

How are you going to show that compassion?

Are there any other times in Scripture when Jesus had compassion on someone?

Mark 1:43–45 says, "Then Jesus sent him on his way with a stern warning: 'Don't tell anyone about this. Instead, go to the priest and let him examine you. Take along the offering required in the law of Moses for those who have been healed of leprosy. This will be a public testimony that you have been cleansed.' But the man went and spread the word, proclaiming to everyone what had happened."

Why do you think Jesus told the man not to tell anyone about his healing?

Why do you think the man did not listen to Jesus?

Would you have told other people or would you have remained quiet?

explore

Psalm 145:8–11 says, "The LORD is merciful and compassionate, slow to get angry and filled with unfailing love. The LORD is good to everyone. He showers compassion on all his creation. All of your works will thank you, LORD, and your faithful followers will praise you. They will speak of the glory of your kingdom; they will give examples of your power."

Challenge
The challenge this week is to read **Mark 4–6**. As you read, draw a comic strip of an event in this passage in the boxes on the next page.

Read this passage before your prayer time this week to remind yourself how compassionate our God is.

—Mark

Just Have Faith

We need to have faith in Jesus.

Engage

Prior to today's passage of Scripture, Jesus performed tons of miracles, and His popularity skyrocketed as a result! Large crowds began to follow Him everywhere He went. As Jesus walked with the multitudes of people, two individuals from the crowd decided to approach Jesus for help.

Check It Out
Read Mark 5:21–43.

Who are the three main characters in this event?

I can know it's true:

1. Faith in Jesus made the woman well. There was a woman in the crowd who had been sick for twelve years. She spent all her money on doctors but no one could make her better. She decided to turn to the one person who she knew could make her well. She had so much faith in Jesus that all she wanted to do was touch Jesus' robe. She sneaked up behind Jesus, touched His robe, and was immediately healed. Was it because Jesus' robe was magic? No. She was healed because she had faith.

2. Faith in Jesus brought Jairus's daughter back to life. Jairus was a synagogue leader and an important man in the community. He had a very sick twelve-year-old daughter at home. He looked for Jesus in the huge crowd and begged Him to heal the little girl. Unfortunately, as Jesus was headed to Jairus's home, He was stopped by the sick woman of twelve years we just discussed. Because of this interruption, Jairus's daughter died before Jesus arrived at his home. Jairus was most likely sad, upset, and scared. Jesus told Jairus, "Don't be afraid. Just have _____." Jesus arrived at Jairus's house soon after, and He brought the girl back to life.

3. Jesus will do miracles in your life when you have faith in Him. Just like Jairus and the woman, Jesus tells us, "Just have faith." When we put our faith in Jesus, He will do some amazing works in our lives. He can heal us from sickness, protect us from danger, deliver us from fears, provide for all our needs, comfort us when we are troubled, free us from sin, bring joy to our lives, and much more!

Question

Reread Mark 5:21–43, and underline one thing that stands out to you.

What is one thing that you underlined?

Mark 5:24–25, and 27 says, "Jesus went with him, and all the people followed, crowding around him. A woman in the crowd had suffered for twelve years with constant bleeding. . . . She had heard about Jesus, so she came up behind him through the crowd and touched his robe."

Why do you think the woman sneaked up behind Jesus instead of just asking Him to heal her?

Mark 5:30 says, "Jesus realized at once that healing power had gone out from him, so he turned around in the crowd and asked, 'Who touched my robe?'"

How did Jesus know the woman touched Him?

Who did Jesus let go into the house where the child was dead?

Mark 5:41 says, "Holding her hand, he said to her, '*Talitha koum*,' which means 'Little girl, get up!'"

What language is *Talitha koum*?

How hard do you think it was for Jairus to have faith in Jesus even after his daughter had died?

How hard is it for you to have faith in Jesus?

What does having faith in Jesus look like in your life?

Matthew 17:20 says, "I tell you the truth, if you had faith even as small as a mustard seed, you could say to this mountain, 'Move from here to there,' and it would move. Nothing would be impossible."

Challenge

Your challenge this week is to read **Mark 7–10**.

While you read, do these three things:

1. Underline what makes people unclean.

2. Circle every place Jesus traveled.

3. In your book, list the unusual ways Jesus healed people in these passages.

Read this verse several times this week until you have it memorized.

On Your Mark, Get Set, Follow Jesus

We are called to pick up our crosses and follow Jesus.

Engage
What is the cost of following Jesus?

Check It Out
Read Mark 8:31–38.

I can know it's true:

1. We can choose to follow Jesus. In Mark 8:34, Jesus says, "If any of you wants to be my follower . . ." There are a lot of people who try to get us to follow them. Some of these people might include movie stars, athletes, friends, or family. They would love for us to talk or act just like them. These people want our attention, money, and time. In addition to people, our interests, sports, or hobbies can distract us from following Jesus. It is up to us who we follow. Jesus wants us to follow Him and nothing else.

2. Jesus continued in Mark 8:34 by saying, "You must turn from your selfish ways, take up your cross, and follow me." Turning from your selfish ways means saying "No" to yourself. Think of some people you say "No" to.

   Jesus tells us to say "No" to ourselves! He asks us to put aside our own wants and desires so we can focus on the needs of others. This is no easy task! We naturally want comfort, popularity, money, power, and so much more. Jesus tells us it is time to stop thinking about ourselves.

3. To have eternal life, we must give up our lives. Mark 8:35 says, "If you try to hang on to your life, you will lose it. But if you give up your life for [Jesus'] sake and for the sake of the Good news, you will save it."

   Does Jesus want us to die on the cross like He did? No, He doesn't. Jesus wants us to have an amazing life here on earth. So what does it mean to "lose your life"? We must give our lives away. Every time we put someone else's needs ahead of ours, we give our lives away. When we show kindness to someone who is unkind, we give our lives away. The more we lose, the more we gain.

   Following Jesus comes with a high cost: our lives. Giving up our lives to Jesus is well worth the reward.

Question

Mark 8:34 says, "Then, calling the crowd to join his disciples, [Jesus] said, 'If any of you wants to be my follower, you must turn from your selfish ways, take up your cross, and follow me.'"

Do you think the cost of following Jesus is too high? Why or why not?

Who are some people in your life who try to get you to follow them?

What are some things in your life that distract you from following Jesus?

What does saying "No" to yourself mean to you?

What are ways you can say "No" to yourself this week?

Mark 9:33–37 says, "After they arrived at Capernaum and settled in a house, Jesus asked his disciples, 'What were you discussing out on the road?' But they didn't answer, because they had been arguing about which of them was the greatest. He sat down, called the twelve disciples over to him, and said, 'Whoever wants to be first must take last place and be the servant of everyone else.' Then he put a little child among them. Taking the child in his arms, he said to them, 'Anyone who welcomes a little child like this on my behalf welcomes me, and anyone who welcomes me welcomes not only me but also my Father who sent me.'"

How does this passage connect with the passage we just studied?

Who is one person you can put before yourself this week?

How are you going to put him or her before yourself?

Challenge

The challenge this week is to read **Mark 10–13**. Do these three things as you read the chapters:

1. Highlight every question asked.

2. Circle the different names people call Jesus.

3. In your book, write the names people called Jesus.

explore

John 10:27–29 says, "My sheep listen to my voice; I know them, and they follow me. I give them eternal life, and they will never perish. No one can snatch them away from me, for my Father has given them to me, and he is more powerful than anyone else. No one can snatch them from the Father's hand."

How does this passage make you feel knowing you are His sheep?

Grapes, Bad Guys, and a Son

Jesus teaches us through parables.

Engage

In **Mark 12:1–2**, Jesus used a parable to teach an important lesson. Let's take a look at this parable and uncover the heavenly meaning of this earthly story.

Check It Out

Read Mark 12:1–12. Underline the different characters in the parable. There are many different characters in this parable. We are going to answer the question:

Who do these characters represent?

I can know it's true:

1. The owner of the vineyard represents God. The parable begins by describing a man who buys a field and prepares it for harvest. He plants the vineyard, builds a wall, digs a pit, and builds a tower. Once everything is ready, the owner rents the field to other farmers. The owner provides everything the renters need in order to have a bountiful harvest.

   Just like the owner provides to the renters, God provides for us. God gives us everything we need in life, and we can trust that He will provide for all our needs.

2. The tenant farmers represent the religious leaders who were rejecting Jesus. The story continues with farmers who rent the vineyard from the owner. When harvest time comes, the owner sends his servants to the farmers to collect what was owed to him. The tenant farmers proceed to beat up and kill several servants who came to collect the money.

After the farmers reject several sets of servants, the owner sends his own son to collect what was due. The farmers decide to reject and kill the owner's own son in hopes of taking over the fields. At the end of the parable, the owner comes back and pronounces judgment on the farmers.

After hearing this parable, the religious leaders in that day were upset, because they knew they were being portrayed as the bad guys in Jesus' story. They were the ones who were going to be judged in the end.

There are many people today who reject Jesus just as the religious leaders did. God, like the land owner in the parable, is patient and gives people many chances. But, in the end, God will judge those who reject His Son.

3. The servants represent the prophets and the son represents Jesus. Throughout the history of Israel, God sent prophets to His people to teach them and warn them of coming judgment. These prophets

were often mistreated and rejected, like the servants in the parable. Examples include Elijah being chased into the wilderness, Isaiah being sawed in two, Zechariah being stoned in the temple, and John the Baptist being beheaded.

In the parable, the owner ultimately decides to send his own son. The farmers mistreat the son the same way they did the servants. Jesus, God's Son, was also rejected and killed. But the parable doesn't end with the death of the son. The owner rents his vineyard to different farmers—ones that would not reject him, his servants, or his son.

Question

Mark 12:3–5 says, "But the farmers grabbed the servant, beat him up, and sent him back empty-handed. The owner then sent another servant, but they insulted him and beat him over the head. The next servant he sent was killed. Others he sent were either beaten or killed."

Why do you think the tenant farmers acted the way they did?

How would you have felt if you were the owner and the first servant you sent out came back beat up and empty-handed?

How many more chances would you have given the farmers?

What would you have done if you were the owner and the farmers killed your son?

Read **Matthew 13:24–30** and **Matthew 13:36–43**.

After reading these passages, how important is it for you to believe in Jesus?

How important is it for you to tell others about Jesus?

- What was the name of the olive grove where Jesus prayed? ◯ ___ ___ ___ ___ ___ ___ ___ ___ ___.
- With what did Judas betray Jesus? ___ ___ ◯ ___.
- What did Jesus call out with a loud voice?

___ ___ ___ ___, ___ ___ ___ ___, ___ ___ ___ ___ ___ ___ ___ ___ ___ ___ ___ ___ ___ ◯ ___?

Challenge

This week's challenge is to read **Mark 14–16**. As you read, answer the questions below. Unscramble the circled letters to finish this sentence: Jesus is the ___ ___ ___ ___ ___   ___ ___ ___.

- Why did the religious leaders not arrest Jesus during the Passover celebration? It would cause a ___ ___ ◯ ___.
- Who did Jesus say will always be among us? ___ ◯ ___ ___.
- What did Jesus break and give to His disciples? ___ ___ ___ ___ ◯.

explore

Jesus says in **Matthew 13:40–41, 43**, "Just as the weeds are sorted out and burned in the fire, so it will be at the end of the world. The Son of Man will send his angels, and they will remove from his Kingdom everything that causes sin and all who do evil. . . . Then the righteous will shine like the sun in their Father's Kingdom. Anyone with ears to hear should listen and understand!"

Read this passage several times this week. Consider what kind of impact this truth has on your life.

Curtains Up

We are no longer separated from God because of Jesus' sacrifice.

Engage

Mark wrote about a curtain that was torn in two when Jesus died. This small detail would have been significant to the original readers of Mark. However, many readers today might not understand the significance of the temple curtain.

Check It Out
Read Mark 15:33–39.

I can know it's true:

1. The curtain represents separation from God. The temple was established as a place for the Israelites to worship to God. Read **Hebrews 9:1–8**.

Because the people were sinful, they did not have the privilege of entering into the Most Holy Place. The Most Holy Place was where God made His presence known. In fact, a large curtain divided this room from the rest of the temple specifically to separate a Holy God from sinful people. The high priest was the only person who could enter and approach the almighty God.

2. Jesus is now our High Priest! When the high priest entered into the Most Holy Place, he would offer a blood sacrifice to cover the sins of the people. These sacrifices had to be made once every year because the animal's blood was not perfect. However, the law changed after Jesus died on the cross. Jesus, a perfect man, offered His own blood to cover the sins of the people. Since the sacrifice was perfect, the high priest no longer had to go behind the curtain to offer imperfect animals. God tore the curtain from top to bottom to show that everyone can have direct access to Him through Jesus. Read **Hebrews 10:19–22**.

3. We are now God's temple! The curtain that separated us from God's presence tore in half, and the old temple was no longer needed. Does that mean God no longer has a temple? No, God has a new temple! God's presence isn't found in a building or in a structure but in the hearts and lives of those who follow Him.

Being God's temple is a great responsibility. Knowing God lives in us should change what we put into our hearts and minds. We should ask ourselves if the things we watch, listen to, and think about are appropriate for God's temple. How amazing is it to know that the holy God is living in you and me! Read **1 Corinthians 3:16** and **Ephesians 2:22**.

Question

Hebrews 10:1–2 says, "The old system under the law of Moses was only a shadow, a dim preview of the good things to come, not the good things themselves. The sacrifices under that system were repeated again and again, year after year, but they were never able to provide perfect cleansing for those who came to worship. If they could have provided perfect cleansing, the sacrifices would have stopped, for the worshipers would have been purified once for all time, and their feelings of guilt would have disappeared."

How would you feel if you had to continually sacrifice animals to receive forgiveness of the things you did wrong?

Why is Jesus' sacrifice considered the ultimate sacrifice?

The curtain in the temple was very large. It was sixty-six feet high, thirty-three feet wide, and about four inches thick. It was so heavy it took about three hundred priests to carry it.

Mark 15:38 says, "And the curtain in the sanctuary of the Temple was torn in two, from top to bottom."

Why do you think Mark added that the curtain was torn from top to bottom?

First Corinthian 3:16 says, "Don't you realize that all of you together are the temple of God and that the Spirit of God lives in you?"

What does it mean that our bodies are now God's temple?

How should knowing we are God's temple affect our lives?

What are you going to change in order to be a better temple for God?

Mark 16:6 says, "But the angel said, 'Don't be alarmed. You are looking for Jesus of Nazareth, who was crucified. He isn't here! He is risen from the dead! Look, this is where they laid his body.'"

Challenge

The challenge for this week is to pick another book of the Bible to read. Create a reading plan for the next several weeks that will help you accomplish your goal. Remember to enjoy reading the Bible and mark different things you find interesting. If you have any questions, write them down and ask your pastor, teacher, or parents if they can help.

Do you believe this passage? Work on memorizing what the angel said this week.

My Bible Reading Certificate

Congratulations on reading through
an entire book of the Bible!

Bible Book: _____

Start Date: _____

End Date: _____

Favorite Story from the Book: _____

**Most Important Lesson
from the Book:** _____